THE VOYAGEUR

MIROLAND IMPRINT 6

Canada

Guernica Editions Inc. acknowledges the support of the Canada Council for the Arts and the Ontario Arts Council. The Ontario Arts Council is an agency of the Government of Ontario.

We acknowledge the financial support of the Government of Canada.
Nous reconnaissons l'appui financier du gouvernement du Canada.

THE VOYAGEUR

JEFF STURGE
STORY

NICK MARINKOVICH
ART

MiroLand
publishers

MIROLAND (GUERNICA)
TORONTO – BUFFALO – LANCASTER (U.K.)
2015

Michael Mirolla
Connie McParland, series editor
Nick Marinkovich, cover and interior book design
Guernica Editions Inc.
1569 Heritage Way, Oakville, ON L6M 2Z7
2250 Military Road, Tonawanda, N.Y. 14150-6000 U.S.A.
www.guernicaeditions.com

Distributors:
University of Toronto Press Distribution,
5201 Dufferin Street, Toronto (ON), Canada M3H 5T8
Gazelle Book Services, White Cross Mills, High Town, Lancaster LA1 4XS U.K.

First edition.
Printed in Canada.

Legal Deposit – Third Quarter
Library of Congress Catalog Card Number: 2015930124
Library and Archives Canada Cataloguing in Publication

Sturge, Jeffrey, author
The voyageur / Jeffrey Sturge ; Nick Marinkovich, illustrator.

(Miroland ; 6)
Issued in print and electronic formats.
ISBN 978-1-77183-032-4 (pbk.).--ISBN 978-1-77183-033-1 (epub).--
ISBN 978-1-77183-034-8 (mobi)

1. Graphic novels. I. Marinkovich, Nick, 1976-, illustrator
II. Title.

PN6733.S78V69 2015 741.5'971 C2015-900296-6
C2015-900297-4

BOOK ONE:

Limits Permitted By The Devil

BILBAO, SPAIN 1608
PEOPLE OF THE BASQUE PROVINCES,
People of

IT IS AN UNDISPUTED FACT THE ACCUSATIONS RESULTING FROM THE WITCH-HUNTS PLAGUING THESE LANDS ARE BASED ENTIRELY ON DECEIT AND SELF-DELUSION.
NO ONE HERE SPOKE OF THE OCCULT UNTIL THE HOLY OFFICE'S PERSECUTION BEGAN. BEFORE THIS, WE KNEW NOTHING ABOUT WITCH SECTS OR EVIL ARTS.

THE UNEDUCATED AND LONELY SOULS DEVIATING FROM THE NORM OF SOCIETY HAVE BEEN THE FIRST TO BE ACCUSED.

BUT NOW IT SEEMS ANYONE WANTING TO SETTLE AN OLD RIVALRY OR GRIEVANCE CAN HAVE HIS NEIGHBOUR PUT TO THE QUESTION, REGARDLESS OF PROOF.
INDEED, THIS GOES BEYOND ALL HUMAN REASON AND MAY EVEN PASS THE LIMITS PERMITTED BY THE DEVIL.

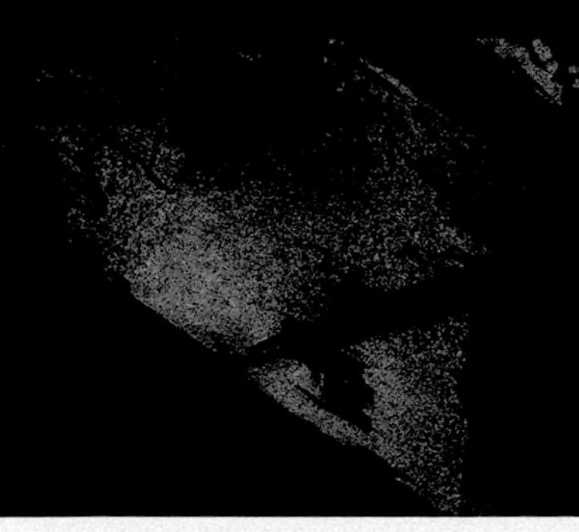

AND A CHURCH THAT SHOULD BE THE VOICE OF REASON SEEKS ONLY TO FAN THE FLAMES OF THIS MADNESS. IT MUST FALL UPON THE PEOPLE TO END THESE SENSELESS ACTS BEFORE EVENTS SLIP BEYOND ALL CONTROL.
C.R

YOU'RE THE PRINT MASTER, YES?
I AM...
NICE PLACE. NO CRUCIFIX THOUGH.
NOT A RELIGIOUS MAN, I GUESS?
MAY I HELP YOU SIR?

MY NAME IS **FATHER ARTURO DE SANDOVAL**.
I'VE HEARD YOU DO GOOD WORK HERE AND WANTED TO ASK ABOUT YOUR RATE.
YOU **HONOR** ME WITH YOUR REQUEST FATHER.
UNFORTUNATELY MY SMALL SHOP IS OVERLOADED AT THE MOMENT. I'M AFRAID I WOULDN'T HAVE THE TIME.

BUT I HAVEN'T EVEN SAID WHAT I WANT.
BESIDES, YOU DON'T LOOK BUSY TO ME.
I'M NOT SURE THAT'S YOUR CONCERN.
MAYBE NOT.
BUT THERE ARE TEN THOUSAND SOULS BEHIND THESE CITY WALLS...
...AND COUNTLESS OTHERS BEYOND...
...CLAIMING TO SUFFER DAILY FROM THE TERROR OF WITCHCRAFT.
AND WHEN PRINTED LETTERS CIRCULATE, TRYING TO UNDERMINE THE INQUISITION INTO THIS MATTER...
...SAYING THERE'S NO... RATIONAL REASON TO BELIEVE IN SUCH THINGS...
...THIS BECOMES MY CONCERN.
I'M NOT SURE WHAT YOU'RE GETTING AT.
NO ONE WOULD BENEFIT MORE FROM CONVINCING US WITCHES DON'T EXIST THAN A WITCH, YES?

YOU'RE ACCUSING ME OF WITCHCRAFT?!
WHAT WOULD I NEED TO PROVE - THAT YOU CAN FLY? THAT YOU CAN PASS THROUGH WALLS OR TURN INTO A CAT?
THIS IS INSANE!
YOU'RE RIGHT, IT'S COMPLETELY INSANE. BUT I DON'T NEED PROVE ANYTHING.
THE PEOPLE ARE SCARED, AND THEY'LL BELIEVE WHAT I TELL THEM.

NOW TO BE HONEST, I DON'T CARE WHAT THEY THINK. WE BOTH KNOW THESE TRIALS ARE A FARCE.
SCARE THE IGNORANT WHILE THE POWERFUL SEIZE THE ESTATES OF THE ACCUSED.
I'M HERE TO ROOT OUT THE REAL DANGER.
IT'S NOW FASHIONABLE FOR CERTAIN YOUNG PEOPLE - WITH NO OUTWARDLY USEFUL TALENT - TO UNEARTH ANCIENT SECRETS LIKE LOGIC AND PHILOSOPHY. THEN USE THEM TO CONDEMN A CHURCH THAT WANTS ONLY TO SAVE THEIR SOULS FROM HELL.

I'VE EVEN TRACED SOME OF THESE TEXTS TO THIS VERY SHOP.

MAKE NO MISTAKE SIR.
UNLIKE MANY WILD ACCUSATIONS THROWN AROUND THESE PARTS, MINE ARE CAREFULLY RESEARCHED.

HERE'S AN EXAMPLE.
A FAMILY CALLED ALBA MOVED HERE SOME TIME AGO.
NOW WHAT'S INTERESTING IS THEIR REAL NAME IS NAGHELA. THEY'RE JEWS YOU SEE, AND CHANGED IT AFTER THE GREAT PURGE.
OF COURSE THE PURGE HAPPENED A HUNDRED YEARS AGO, BUT FORTUNATELY SOME PEOPLE KEEP TRACK OF THESE THINGS.
NOW SINCE JEWS CAN'T LEGALLY OWN PROPERTY, I ASSUME THEY'RE RENTING IN THE EASTERN QUARTER. BUT LIKE YOU, I'VE BEEN VERY BUSY AND HAVEN'T HAD TIME TO CHECK.

LOOK... I'M NO RADICAL.
I ONLY PRINTED WHAT WAS PAID FOR.
BUT YOU KNOW WHO I'M TALKING ABOUT, YES?
FATHER?
WAIT.
I WANT YOU TO WATCH THEM FOR ME.
GET A LIST OF NAMES AND WHERE THEY MEET.
I'M SURE YOU'LL FIND THE TIME IN YOUR BUSY SCHEDULE.

YOU'RE LATE, MARCO.
SORRY FATHER, BUT SOMETHING'S COME UP. LET'S TALK OVER HERE.
THE LITTLE BIRD SAYS SHE'S LOCATED THE KEY.
SO?
WE'VE GOTTEN A DOZEN FALSE LEADS THIS PAST MONTH.
SHE SENT THIS.
DON'T DO ANYTHING YET.
THERE'S SOMEONE I NEED TO TALK TO.
AND THE PRINTER?
LEAVE HIM.
FOR NOW.

WATERFORD, IRELAND
CAREFUL NOW.
YOU DON'T WANT IT TO FLARE INTO YOUR EYES.
PISS OFF RUARI!

I'VE DONE THIS BEFORE IN CASE YOU FORGOT.
OKAY, READY.

FIRE!
GOOD MAN!
UH... THANKS.
NICE SHOT FINTAN!

I DIDN'T KNOW YOU WERE A *MARKSMAN.*
ARE YOU *KIDDING?*
THIS BOY IS MY *STAR PUPIL!*
HOW *EXCITING!*

WHEN I'M DONE, FINTAN WILL BE ABLE SHOOT A CHERRY OFF THAT PRETTY LITTLE HEAD WITHOUT HARMING A HAIR.
NOW IN THE MEANTIME, IF YOU WANNA SEE A REALLY *GREAT* SHOT...

HEY!
LOOK NO FURTHER...
...THAN THE MOST FEARED MUSKET MAN...
...IN DON GIOVANNI DE MEDICI'S GREAT COMPANY OF MERCENARIES.

BRILLIANT!
WHY DON'T YOU COME BACK LATER GIRLS?
NOUS VOUS MONTRERONS COMMENT DECHARGER DES **GRANDES ARMES**.

DID YOU JUST SAY WE'D SHOW THEM HOW TO FIRE A BIG GUN?
NOT BAD. YOUR FRENCH IS GETTING AS GOOD AS YOUR AIM.

THAT WENT WELL, EH?
FOR YOU MAYBE.

WHAT'RE YA TALKING ABOUT?
THAT ONE COULDN'T TAKE HER EYES OFF YOU.

SHE WAS LOOKING AT YOU, EEJIT.
DON'T BE LIKE THAT, CUZ. SHE JUST NEVER KNEW YOU WERE A GUNSLINGER.
WOMEN LIKE A DANGEROUS MAN. I COULD TELL YOU SOME STORIES FROM MY TIME IN FRANCE AND THE EMPIRE.
I'VE HEARD THEM ALL.
I'LL HAVE MORE PRETTY SOON, ONCE I HEAD BACK OVER.
BUT YOU'VE ONLY BEEN HERE A FEW MONTHS.
YEAH WELL, THERE'S SOMETHING I NEED TO ***TAKE CARE*** OF.
WHAT'S IMPORTANT ENOUGH TO DRAG YOU ALL THE WAY BACK THERE?

I SPENT FIVE YEARS FIGHTING ALONGSIDE A PRETTY MEAN BUNCH OF GUYS.
I DID A LOT OF **BAD** STUFF.
THINGS I CAN'T **LET GO** OF.
AND IT'S GETTING **WORSE** NOW...
...BACK HERE...
...WITH TIME TO **THINK** ABOUT IT.

WHAT SORT OF STUFF?
I BET IT'S GOT SOMETHING TO DO WITH THAT WEIRD **COIN** YOU KEEP FIDDLING WITH.
MAYBE IT DOES. YOU SHOULD COME OVER WITH ME AND FIND OUT.
HE'S NOT GOING ANYWHERE.

AUNTIE!
ALWAYS A TREAT TO BASK IN YOUR RADIANCE.
AND YOU'RE AS CHARMING AS YOUR DEADBEAT UNCLE. NOW GET OUT OF HERE.

I WAS HELPING HIM.
WITH LESSONS IN WOMEN AND GUNS? VERY USEFUL FOR A FARMER.

WHO SAYS HE HAS TO WORK ON A FARM?

I TOLD YOU BEFORE, HE'S NOT LIKE YOU. I DIDN'T SPENT FIFTEEN YEARS RAISING HIM SO HE COULD DIE IN SOME FOREIGN WAR.

RIGHT THEN, CUZ. HAVE FUN SLOPPING THE PIGS.
SEE YA GORGEOUS.

ARSEHOLE.

WELL?
ARE YOU GOING TO STAND THERE OR DO SOME WORK?
YEAH YEAH...

OFFICE OF THE INQUISITION,
BILBAO

IS IT DAY OR NIGHT?

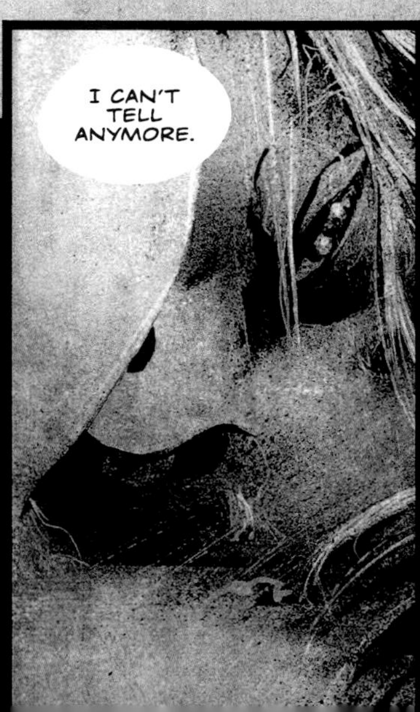
I CAN'T TELL ANYMORE.

I HARDLY EVEN REMEMBER YOUR FACE.
I WAS SOMEONE IMPORTANT ONCE...
WASN'T I?
CROWDS OF PEOPLE CAME TO HEAR ME.
BUT I'VE NOT SPOKEN TO ANYONE IN SO LONG.

THERE'S YOU...

BUT YOU NEVER STAY.

AND THEN THERE'S...
...HIM...

HELLO GIORDANO.
WHAT DO YOU WANT?

I WANT YOU TO COOPERATE, THAT'S ALL.

I FEED YOU, DON'T I?
GIVE YOU A WARM PLACE TO SLEEP, YES?

YOU'VE DRIVEN ME MAD.

YOU'RE IN A BAD MOOD.
THAT'S UNFORTUNATE.

YOU WANT TO KNOW WHAT I DID TODAY, HUH? I VISITED A FRIEND WHO RUNS A PRINT SHOP.
YOU'VE SEEN THESE MACHINES, YES? THEY CAN PRINT THREE THOUSAND COPIES IN A DAY.
UNBELIEVABLE.
THERE WAS A TIME WHEN A MONK WOULD SPEND HALF HIS LIFE WRITING OUT A BIBLE.
THE THOUGHT OF HORDES OF CRACKPOTS AND AGITATORS SENDING THEIR IDEAS OUT TO THE MASSES, IT DRIVES ME MAD.
NO OFFENCE.
YOU KNOW THE INVENTOR OF THE PRINTING PRESS WAS A GOLDSMITH, YES?
HIS KNOWLEDGE OF METAL ALLOWED HIM TO REALIZE IT WAS THE BEST STUFF FOR CREATING DURABLE TYPE.
AS I UNDERSTAND IT, HE LEARNED THIS FROM MINTING COINS.

OH, AND I ALSO LEARNED WHERE THE *KEY* IS.

I'VE TOLD YOU A HUNDRED TIMES I KNOW NOTHING ABOUT A KEY.

YOU REMEMBER THE NIGHT I FOUND YOU HALF-DEAD IN THAT ALLEY?

YOU SAID THERE WAS JUST YOU AND THE TWO MEN WE FOUND WITH YOU.
THERE WAS SOMEONE ELSE THOUGH, WASN'T THERE?

HE STOLE THE KEY AND LEFT YOU, YES?

WELL GUESS WHAT?

HE'S LEARNED YOU'RE ALIVE. AND HE THINKS YOU'RE AFTER HIM.
HE'S MOVING AGAINST YOU GIORDANO.

THAT'S A *LIE*.
YOU'RE *LYING*!

BUT I KNOW HE'S AN *IRISHMAN,* DON'T I?

WHAT WOULD YOU SAY IF I TOLD YOU HE'S PLANNING TO GO AFTER...

...YOUR *DAUGHTER?*

OH!
LOOK WHAT I'VE DONE!

I KNOW WHAT YOU'RE THINKING.
NO ONE COULD KNOW ABOUT HER, YES?
I ALMOST DIDN'T - YOU HID HER SO WELL.

THE WORLD THINKS YOU'RE DEAD GIORDANO.
YOU'RE GOING TO ROT IN THIS TOWER.
BUT I CAN SAVE HER.
PLEASE.
LEAVE ME ALONE.

SEE.
I CAN FIND OUT ANYTHING I NEED TO.
THIS IS HIM ISN'T IT.
HE STOLE THE KEY AND LEFT YOU, YES?
NO... WHY WOULD HE DO THIS?
I'LL KILL HIM!
THANK YOU.

WHAT? YOU DIDN'T KNOW?
I NEEDED TO BE SURE.
YOU TRICKED ME.

YOU WERE A VALUABLE ALLY ONCE.

IF ONLY YOU STAYED ON THE RIGHT SIDE.

N... NOOO!

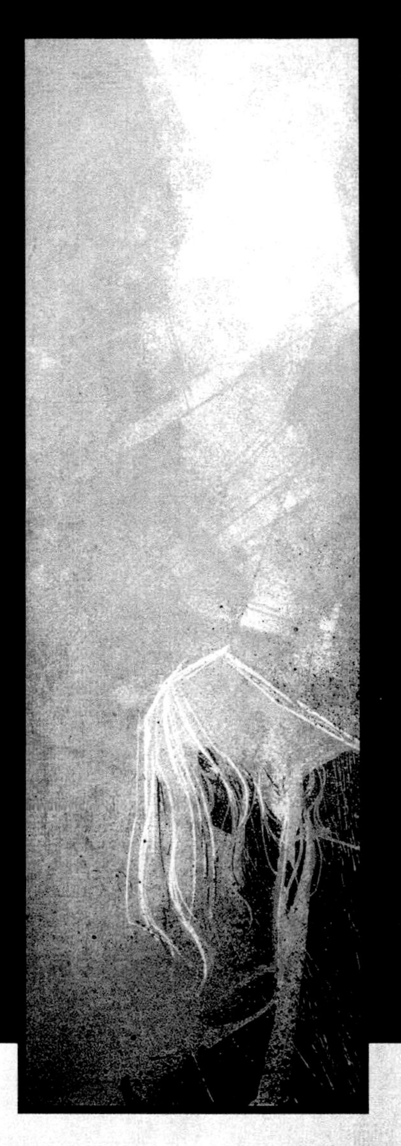

FINTAN'S FARM,
WATERFORD

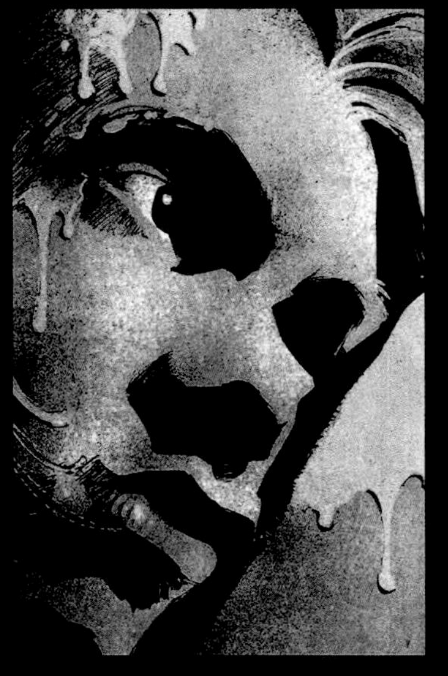

[SIGH]

THANKS.

MUSKET COMPANY READY!

AIM.

FIRE!

HEY FINTAN!

I HEAR YOU'RE A GOOD SHOT WITH A GUN.
WE'RE GOING TO THE HARVEST DANCE. ARE YOU?
WELL I...
THE ONLY THING HE'LL BE DANCING WITH TONIGHT IS THAT PITCHFORK.
JUST AS WELL. NO ONE COULD TELL IF HE'S A BOY OR A GIRL ANYWAY WITH THAT HAIR.
WHAT'S WRONG?
YOUR DRUNK DADDY STEAL YOUR TONGUE BEFORE HE WALKED OUT?

HA! SEE YA, MOPE.
HAH!
PUT DOWN THE STONES, LITTLE COCKSUCKER.
LET'S SEE HOW TOUGH YOU ARE.

BOLLOCKS.
GET THE HELL AWAY FROM ME!!!
COME ON. LET'S JUST GO TO THE DANCE.
I'LL SEE YOU LATER.

THE PRINTSHOP,
BILBAO

NEVER KNOWN YOU TO BE SO CARELESS, MASTER.
GOOD THING I'M EARLY.
YOU WANT A *FIGHT*, PRIEST?
COME GET ME.
???

CAREFUL WHAT YOU WISH FOR SUNSHINE.

SORRY MATE.
THE BOSS'S BEEN CALLED AWAY IN A HURRY...
...AND HE'S CHARGED OLD MARCO HERE WITH TYING UP THE LOOSE ENDS.
I'M PRETTY GOOD AT THAT.

ASK ME...
KILLING YOU RADICALS IS LIKE CUTTING THE HEAD OFF A HYDRA.
ONE GETS CHOPPED...
...AND TWO MORE POP UP.

FEN'S FORGE, WATERFORD
LET ME SHOW YOU HOW IT'S DONE LADS.
YEAH!
I'D SAY THAT'S A NEW RECORD.

NOW YOU SHOULD HAVE SEEN THE BODIES I WAS THROWING AROUND THE EMPIRE.
SURE RUARI. YOU'RE A HARD MAN.
HERE WE GO.
OUR TINY COMPANY TOOK OUT SIX HUNDRED OF THE EMPEROR'S MEN.
IT WAS FIVE HUNDRED LAST TIME.
YOU CALLING ME A *LIAR*, GILLY?
I FOUGHT MY WAY FROM PARIS TO ROME WHILE YOU'VE JUST BEEN SITTIN' HERE ON YOUR ASS.
YOU'RE NOTHING BUT A *THUG*.

I'VE SEEN YOUR KIND, BOUGHT OVER TO KINSALE BY THE ENGLISH. YOU FIGHT FOR MONEY, BUT YOU'VE GOT NO *HONOUR*.
AT LEAST I GET *PAID*.
WHAT DO YOU GOT TO SHOW FOR ALL YOUR PATRIOTIC PISS BUT A COUPLE OF DEAD BROTHERS?
YOU'RE LUCKY I'M NOT TEN YEARS YOUNGER. I'D SPLIT YOUR HEAD OPEN.
NOT ON YOUR BEST DAY.
WHAT THE HELL IS WRONG WITH YOU?
HE STARTED IT.
DIDN'T HE ROOSTER?
GET OUT OF HERE RUARI.
I'M SICK OF YOU SKULKING AROUND LOOKING FOR A FIGHT.
XXX

YOU THINK I GOT NOWHERE ELSE TO GO?

!
I'M LEAVING THIS DUMP OF AN ISLAND THE FIRST CHANCE I GET.

RIGHT ROOSTER?

NOT A CHANCE, ROOSTER.
NOT A CHANCE.

[ZZZ]
BACK AT FINTAN'S

LIKE ROCKS, DO YA?

EH, COCK SUCKER?

YOU GOT TO THE COUNT OF THREE BEFORE I BLOW A HOLE IN YER FACE.
JESUS!
RUARI?
WHAT'S GOING ON?

THIS BOY WAS GOING TO **SMASH** YOUR FACE IN.
I THINK WE SHOULD SMASH ***HIS***.
PLEASE...
MAYBE WE SHOULD LET HIM GO.
YOU'RE A KINDER MAN THAN ME, CUZ.
YEAH, WELL.
THANKS FOR SAVING MY FACE.
ANYWAY, HOW COME YOU'RE NOT AT THAT HARVEST DANCE?
GOD KNOWS YOU COULD USE SOME PRACTICE TALKING TO GIRLS.
LISTEN, YOU NEED TO START THINKING ABOUT ***YOURSELF***.
I GOTTA GET BACK TO WORK. CAN'T BELIEVE I FELL ASLEEP. MA'S GONNA KILL ME.

HEY!
THAT DODGY BOOZER WHERE YOU GO TO DRINK AND FIGHT?
NO THANKS.
COME TO THE PUB WITH ME. WE'LL HAVE A FEW JARS, PLAY SOME GAMES.

LOOK...
...HANGING OUT WITH YOU AND TEACHING YOU A FEW THINGS...
IT'S MADE ME SEE I'M NOT TOTALLY ROTTEN. AND IT'S GOT A LOT TO DO WITH WHY I'M GOING BACK.
I REALLY WANT TO TALK TO YOU. I'LL HELP YOU FINISH THIS AFTER. PROMISE.

[SIGH]

FINE.

THE BUNCH OF GRAPES TAVERN,
NEAR WATERFORD
DON'T TELL YOUR MOTHER I BROUGHT YOU HERE.

TWO ALES, SIR!
YOU'RE OUT LATE, LITTLE FELLA.

THIS ISLAND. NOTHING BUT COWS, SHEEP AND TURNIPS.
PRETTY SAD ISN'T IT.
IT BLOODY SUCKS!
LIKE I SAID, YOU SHOULD COME WITH ME.
IS THAT WHAT THIS IS ABOUT?
IF IT IS I'M NOT INTERESTED.

HOW DO YOU KNOW? YOU'VE NEVER BEEN FIVE MILES FROM YOUR HOUSE.
YOU THINK I'M SCARED?
HA! EASY BIG MAN. I NEVER SAID THAT.
BUT THERE'S MORE TO LIFE THAN BREAKING YOUR BACK IN A FIELD.
CHEERS.
I COULDN'T LEAVE MA ON HER OWN.
YOU'D MAKE ENOUGH COIN WITH ME THAT SHE'D NEVER HAVE TO WORK AGAIN.
COME ON, I'LL SHOW YOU.
KEEP YOUR EYE ON THE SHELL!

AW, TOO BAD!
HARD LUCK MY MAN. ANYONE ELSE?
OVER HERE.

CERTAINLY SIR. HAVE A SEAT. WHAT ARE WE WAGERING TONIGHT?
LET'S SEE...
I'LL PUT IT UP AGAINST EVERYTHING YOU GOT THERE.
I'VE NEVER SEEN THIS UH... CURRENCY BEFORE.
!!!
SO WHAT?
THOSE ARE SOME SHELLS YOU SCROUNGED OFF A BEACH, AND THAT'S A SOLID GOLD COIN.
NOW DO YOU WANT TO PLAY FOR SOME REAL MONEY OR NOT?

LET'S GO.
ARE YOU MAD?
HE'S CHEATING.
RELAX. I KNOW WHAT I'M DOING.
THAT ONE.

AWW, TOO BAD.
I GUESS...
GLRRRP!
SON OF A BITCH!

GRAB HIM!
THANKS PAL.

ZE SHERIFF'S COMING!
GET YOUR FRIEND OUT OF 'ERE!
NO! STOP! GLRRK...!

JESUS RUARI! WHAT THE HELL?!
COME ON!
AW SHYTE, IT'S THE SHERIFF!
THAT GIRL'S WITH HIM.
WHAT GIRL?
QUICK, DOWN HERE.

THIS IS REALLY BAD, ISN'T IT?!
YEAH, IT'S NOT GOOD. I SHOULDN'T A DONE THAT.
BUT THE LITTLE ***BASTARD!*** RUNNING OFF WITH MY MONEY...
WHAT HAPPENS IF THEY CATCH YOU? WILL YOU ***HANG***?

MAYBE.
LOOKS LIKE WE'LL BE HEADING OUT SOONER THAN I THOUGHT.
WE?
YOU WERE THE ONE WHO GRABBED HIM. YOU THINK THAT CROWD OF DRUNKS BACK THERE WON'T TELL THE SHERIFF?

I DIDN'T KNOW YOU WERE GOING TO CUT HIS BLOODY THROAT OUT!
LOOK, I'M SORRY. BUT IT'LL JUST BE FOR A LITTLE WHILE.
HE WAS A SCUMBAG ANYWAY. IT'LL BLOW OVER IN A YEAR OR SO.
A YEAR?!

JUST CALM DOWN.
HERE'S YOUR SHARE FROM TONIGHT, BY THE WAY. SHOULD BE ABOUT TWENTY CROWNS.

LIKE I SAID, THERE'S MORE TO LIFE THAN BREAKING YOUR BACK IN A FIELD.
YOU'LL SEE WHEN YOU COME WITH ME. WE'RE GONNA MAKE A GREAT TEAM.
RUARI O'NEILL!
STAY WHERE YOU ARE!

QUICK, LET'S MAKE A RUN FOR THE WOODS!
IT'S TOO FAR.
THAT FAT LITTLE PRICK COULD EASILY RUN US DOWN ON HIS HORSE.
BUT WHAT DO WE DO? I'M NOT GOING TO THE **GALLOWS** RUARI!
GET OUTTA HERE. DON'T GO HOME, STAY IN THE WOODS. MEET ME BACK HERE AT DAWN.
BUT WHAT'LL HAPPEN TO YOU?
I'VE BEEN IN A HUNDRED SCRAPES WORSE THAN THIS. DON'T WORRY, JUST GET OUTTA HERE.
GO!

SHERIFF!
NICE ANIMAL. YOUR PRIZE FOR GETTING CROWNED HARVEST QUEEN AGAIN?
WHERE'S THAT KID THAT WAS WITH YOU?
NOT SURE WHO YOU MEAN EXACTLY.
WHATEVER, IT DOESN'T MATTER.
JUST FIND IT.
WAIT, WHAT'S GOIN' ON HERE?

THAT'S NOT IT. IT'S SOME SORT OF COIN.
WHERE'S THAT STUPID ERRAND GIRL GONE? SHE KNOWS.

COIN?
YOU WERE FLASHING AROUND EARLIER. WHERE'D YOU PUT IT?

ENOUGH!
HEY!
STOP!
IN THE NAME OF THE KING!

YOUR KING CAN CRAWL UP MY HOLE.
NOW WHO SENT YOU?
S..STAY BACK OR I'LL SHOOT!
WHO SENT YOU?!

RUARI!

OOOMPFF!
OW! OW! GET OFF ME!
COME ON.

YOU LITTLE BASTARD! I'LL FIND OUT WHERE YOU LIVE!
AGHH!
GET UP!
THEY'RE GETTING AWAY!

HOW WELL CAN YOU RIDE A HORSE?
NOT WELL.

WE GOTTA KEEP GOING.
PUT ME DOWN.
JESUS ARSEHOLE! WILL YOU PUT ME DOWN?

SORRY FINTAN.
I REALLY MESSED UP THIS TIME.
I TOOK THIS OFF A MAN I WAS HIRED TO PROTECT AND LEFT HIM FOR DEAD.
NOW THE MEN WHO WERE AFTER HIM ARE AFTER ME...
...AND YOU TOO.

BUT I DON'T KNOW *ANYTHING* ABOUT THAT STUPID COIN!
IT DOESN'T MATTER.
THEY'VE SEEN YOUR FACE.
THEY'LL KILL YOU WITHOUT A SECOND THOUGHT.

YOU'VE GOT TO GET OUT OF HERE FINTAN.
AND TAKE THIS WITH YOU. THEY CAN'T FIND IT ON ME.
I DON'T WANT IT.
I WANT TO GO HOME.
LISTEN TO ME.
RIGHT NOW THIS COIN'S YOUR ONLY CHANCE OF STAYING ALIVE.
FIND DAVID CHOKE IN WATERFORD HARBOUR.
EVERY SECOND WEEK, HE MAKES A RUN TO LE HAVRE IN FRANCE. SHOW HIM THE COIN AND GET ON HIS BOAT.
TELL HIM TO GET YOU ON A CARAVAN HEADING TO PARIS.

WHEN YOU GET THERE FIND MY OLD CAPTAIN, *FARINATA UBERTI*.
TELL HIM BRUNO'S ALIVE AND YOU NEED TO FIND HIM.
UNDERSTAND?
THE COIN'S GOT TO GET BACK TO **BRUNO.**
IF YOU WANT TO STAY ALIVE...
...YOU'LL DO WHAT I TOLD YOU...
...NOW GET...
...OUT...
...OF...
...HERE.

RUARI?

GAAHH!...

JESUS, HE'S *DEAD!*
I'VE GOT TO GIVE THEM THE COIN AND HOPE THIS WHOLE THING *ENDS.*
BUT I'VE NEVER SEEN RUARI SO SERIOUS.
WHAT IF HE'S RIGHT AND THEY KILL ME TOO?
BOY, I'M FEELING LIGHT-HEADED ALL OF A SUDDEN.
GOTTA SIT, JUST FOR A SECOND...

JUST FOR A...

TO BE CONTINUED...

ACKNOWLEDGEMENTS

The Voyageur could not have happened without the generous support – and patience – of our family and friends. A special thanks to those who helped us along the way.

From Jeff:

Hannah Waisberg, Eliot & Harry Sturge, Jean and Cyril Sturge, Lesleigh Sturge, Larry Bambrick, Radek Zuraweicki, Chris Gagosz, Chris Blow, Lorie Waisberg, Ginny Bellwood, Adrian Tucker, Jeff Hirschfield and Fraser Clarke.

From Nick:

Gojko and Katerina Marinkovich, Mei-Lin & William Chen, Steven Fernando, Kelly Jankovich, Nicolette Marinkovich, Steve Marinkovich, Craig Small, Alex Jansen, Herman Mcleod and Ajay Handa.

And, a very special note to Hui-an, Zoey and Nathan Marinkovich for everything.

As well, we'd like to acknowledge the financial support of all our Kickstarter backers, each of whom helped bring the book to life.

3KOF®
Aaron McMahan
Adam Boreham
Adriana Taseva
Agent Paper
Ainsley Higgins
Ajay & Munira Handa
Alan Friggieri
Alan Liu
Albert Tam
Alberto Casu
Alex Jansen
Alice Donovan
Andrew Raftis
Andrew McKendry
Angela Shayer
Angella Mackey & Kate Hartman
Antonio A Rodriguez
Arthur E. Orneck
Asanga Mallikage
Auspex Publishing
Autopanda
Xavier Baldacci
Ben Russell
Boro Marinkovich
Brad Collins
Brendan Braybrook
Bruce MacKeen
Cameron Jarvis
Cheryl Fisher
Chris Pickle
Christine Alexiou
Colin Moore
Colleen McKim
Craig Small
Crawford
Crystal Middaugh
Diane Jankovich

Daniel Duffin
Danny O'Regan
David Donovan
David J Kehoe
David Levine
Don Fagan
Emily Dragon
Eric Damon Walters
Eric Graves
Eric Mullarky
Erik Augustsson
Erin Breen
Fabio Bondi
Farhan Quadri
Frank Wall
Fraser Clarke
Gavin Maher
Gerard Lahey
Greg Gransden
Greg Trevino
Hannah Waisberg
Herman McLeod
Hubert G. Hutton
Jan Vodicka
Janet and Dave Parsons
Janet and Seamus O'Regan
Jason Gilmore
Jean Sturge
Jeffrey Hirschfield
Jessica Gadling
John Bojtos
John MacLeod
John Otworth
Julian Goddard
Goyko & Katerina Marinkovich
Kathy Mackey
Keith Collier
Kelly Jankovich

Khai Huynh
Kris Olafson
Kushan Fernando
Kyla Springall
Lesleigh Sturge
Laura Knight
Laurette Paterson
Leigh Mackey
Lexi Sprague
Lorie Waisberg
Magnus Harwiss
Mary Feehan
Mei-Lin Chen
Mel G Catre
Micahel o'donoghue
Michael Kot
Michael Sheehan
Michele-Pahtrizio Rossi
Ming Leung
Nadine Giguere
Neil Seneviratne
Nerissa daley
Nicola Defina
Nicolas Munoz
Nicole Campbell
Nicole Visscher Novakovics
Nicolette Savic
Noah Waisberg
Noda Kouniakis
Opal Consulting Inc.
Pascal Tremblay
Pasquale Caruso
Patrick Ellis
Paul Wynen
Peter Kavanagh
Peter Polivka
Peter Russell
Peter Walters

Peter Zukowski
Phil Desjardins
Phil Wall
Pryce Duncalf
Quoc-Nghi Tran
Ramona Lundrigan Sturge
Randy Dodge
Robert Carnel
Robert Eaton
Robin G. LaBelle
Ruwan Jayasinghe
Ryan MacLean
Ryan Quint
Satish Ramburn
Scott Hsieh
Shae Sveniker
Shane Miller
Simon Welykanycz
Snehal Belgaumkar
SODY
Stephanie Carey
Steve Marinkovich
Steve Martin
Sumit Sharan
Suzi Ashworth
Sylvia Mioduszewska
Thomas H.
Tin-An Chen
Tomas Burgos-Caez
Tony Contento
Tu-Anh Ly
Under Belly Comics
Vanessa Jubenot
Véronique Dumas
Vikas Girdhar
William Cusick
Yu-Chun Chen
Zoey & Nathan Marinkovich

AUTHORS

Jeff Sturge

In 1998, after graduating university with a degree in archaeology, Jeff moved from St. John's, Newfoundland to Dublin, where he honed his interest and expertise in Irish history before moving to Toronto.

His career as a TV screenwriter spans the past 10 years. Starting when he successfully pitched an original idea – a show called Stealing Mary – to History Television. He's subsequently written numerous shows – mostly for history and crime-based series – for broadcasters like National Geographic, Discovery Channel, A&E and History.

Nick Marinkovich

Nick is a Canadian illustrator, graphic novelist and conceptual artist, working in publishing, film and video games. He has released titles under Marvel, IDW, Image and Devils Due.

Nick's notable published works include Sony Pictures Underworld, Underworld – Red in Tooth and Claw, Impaler, Nightwolf and the Marvel webcomic When The Hulk Attacks.

In 2010 Nick released the critically acclaimed graphic novel Kenk: A Graphic Portrait, a biography on the notorious Toronto bicycle thief. Kenk was the top selling literary graphic novel of 2010 in Canada.